Birmingham and the Heart of England

Compiled by
Dennis and Jan Kelsall

JARROLD

0711 724237 2729 6B

Acknowledgements

We are grateful for information and advice offered by the Footpath and Rights of Way Officers in the counties encompassed within this guide.

Text: Dennis and Jan Kelsall
Photography: Dennis and Jan Kelsall
Editors: Crawford Gillan, Sonya Calton
Designer: Sarah Crouch

Jarrold Publishing ISBN 7117-2423-7

While every care has been taken to ensure the accuracy of the route directions, the publishers cannot accept responsibility for errors or omissions, or for changes in details given. The countryside is not static: hedges and fences can be removed, field boundaries can alter, footpaths can be rerouted and changes in ownership can result in the closure or diversion of some concessionary paths. Also, paths that are easy and pleasant for walking in fine conditions may become slippery, muddy and difficult in wet weather, while stepping-stones across rivers and streams may become impassable.

If you find an inaccuracy in either the text or maps, please write or e-mail to Jarrold Publishing at one of the addresses below.

First published 2003
by Jarrold Publishing

Printed in Belgium
by Proost NV, Turnhout. 1/03

Jarrold Publishing
Pathfinder Guides, Whitefriars, Norwich NR3 1TR
E-mail: info@totalwalking.co.uk
www.totalwalking.co.uk

Front cover: Canal boat on the Trent & Mersey Canal
Previous page: Baddesley Clinton Church

Contents

Keymap 1

SCALE 1:357 143 or 1 INCH to about 5¾ MILES *1CM to 3.5KM*

| 0 | 2 | 4 | 6 | 8 | 10 KILOMETRES | 15 |

| 0 | 2 | 4 | 6 | MILES 8 | 10 |

KEYMAP HEIGHTS SHOWN IN FEET

Keymap 2

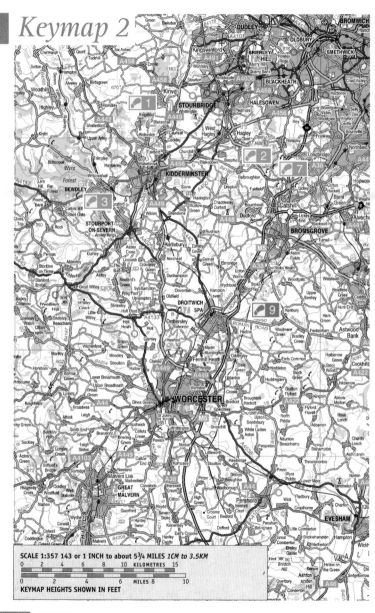

SCALE 1:357 143 or 1 INCH to about 5¾ MILES *1CM to 3.5KM*

KILOMETRES

MILES

KEYMAP HEIGHTS SHOWN IN FEET

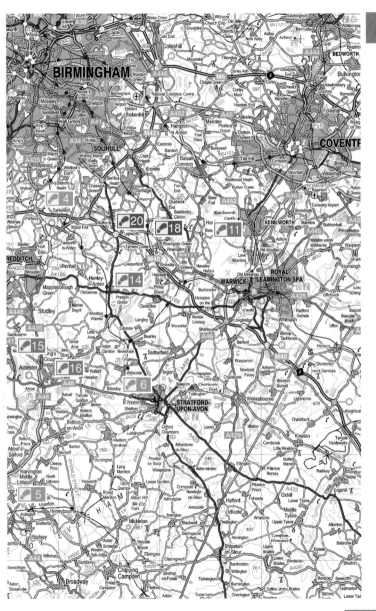

Introduction

It is said that all roads lead to Rome, but glance at any map of England and it looks as if they all radiate from Birmingham. About as far from the sea as you can get, it has grown to become one of England's largest and most prosperous cities. Yet, despite the spread of urbanisation, there is, by contrast, a vast amount of unspoiled countryside within easy reach of the city centre.

The counties immediately surrounding the industrial and commercial heart, Staffordshire, Shropshire, Worcestershire and Warwickshire harbour some of the most agreeable countryside in Britain. Rolling agrarian landscapes spread out at the foot of abrupt hills and escarpments, from whose airy tops are fine views across distant plains enhanced by scattered woods and winding rivers.

This collection of walks seeks out the many facets of the countryside and reveals a wealth of diversity, both natural and man-made. Choose a clear day and wander onto the heights of the Clent Hills or Kinver Edge, and for relatively little physical effort, you will be rewarded by views that stretch as far as the eye can see. Elsewhere, idyllic pathways follow the meanderings of the many rivers and streams that course the landscape, such as the Severn at Hampton Loade and Bewdley or the Alne near Alcester. Some landscapes are not what they seem. Much of Cannock Chase, for example, was, at the beginning of the 20th century, a desolate heath, scarred by the grimy business of mining. The extensive timber stands we see today were only established between the two World Wars, although the area had been naturally forested in antiquity. In other places, and sometimes surprisingly close to modern urbanisation, like at Sutton Park and Earlswood Lakes, there are vestiges of the ancient woodland that once covered much of England and which today support a rich variety of both plant and wildlife.

Farming and the Land

Agriculture has long been an economic mainstay of the region, and in many places, for example around Middle Littleton and Hanbury, ancient ploughing patterns are preserved in the lines of ridges and hollows that corrugate the fields. But it is the enclosures of later centuries, designed to improve efficiency and production, that often underlie the land patterns of today. Yet not all enclosures were made with an eye to profit, and vast landscaped parklands, such as those at Dudmaston and Shugborough, were created to enhance the extravagant country residences of the land-owning classes. Castles and stately homes are to be found throughout the area, from the enigmatic ruins of Kenilworth to the grandeur of Shugborough. And there are more humble residences, too: the rock shelters of Kinver Edge and the quaint cottage that was home to Mary Arden before she married a certain John Shakespeare to whom she presented a son.

Industry in the Villages

Even in Shakespeare's day, industry was important, not in big factories, but in village cottages and small workshops. Gloves, hats, pins and small metal goods were produced in huge quantities. Countless mills grew beside the rivers to power hammers, saws and wheels as well as grind the wheat produced in the fields.

The Great Transport Revolution

The 18th century saw not only great changes in agriculture, but also a revolution in industry, with the discovery of a method to produce iron using coke and the invention of the steam engine. But the massive increase in production could never have been attained without an efficient transport system, the canals; and nowhere in the country was the rapid expansion of waterways more prolific than in the Midlands. The canals brought prosperity, even the farms through which they meandered found a new fast means to convey their produce to the hungry markets. Although the canals declined with the later development of the railways, some still carried cargo until the late 1940s. Today, they are again busy with the passage of brightly coloured boats, winding through some of the area's most beautiful countryside. Their banks and margins, often relatively ignored by modern farming practice, have become refuges for all manner of plant and wildlife. The towpaths offer fine, easy walking, and several of these walks take advantage of this extensive network.

1 *Kinver Edge*

START Below Redcliff outside Kinver
DISTANCE 2½ miles (4km)
TIME 1¾ hours
PARKING Roadside car park on Kingsford Lane by junction with Compton Road
ROUTE FEATURES Undulating woodland paths, but with some steep sections

Protected by the National Trust since 1917, the summit of Kinver Edge offers one of the finest panoramas in the area. This walk onto the hilltop begins through delightful woodland below the cliff, passing an ancient rock shelter, once used as a dwelling. More cave houses are passed on the return, some of which were still occupied until the 1950s.

With your back to the road, bear right into the woodland, following a rising path, initially marked 'Staffordshire Way'. Where the gradient eases at a fork, keep ahead, but at the next fork take the left branch. Shortly, you will reach a crossing track, follow that left. At the next junction higher up, a path joins from the right, and you are then faced with three paths ahead. Fork right over a rise, dropping to a stepped path, the way then winding and undulating at the foot of Kinver Edge. Ignore a path later leaving on the right and keep going until you reach an impressive cave, Nanny's Rock.

Kinver's caves have been lived in for centuries, those at **Holy Austin Rock** taking their name from the belief that a 16th-century hermit, an Augustine friar, used one as his cell. The soft sandstone is easily excavated and natural hollows were extended to provide rooms and cupboards within the hillside, while bricks were used to create windows and doorways at the front. During the 18th century, a booming iron industry attracted workers, and at one time, a dozen families had their homes here.

PUBLIC TRANSPORT Bus service to Kinver (½ mile/800m)
REFRESHMENTS Choice of pubs in Kinver (½ mile/800m)
PUBLIC TOILETS In Kinver (½ mile/800m)
ORDNANCE SURVEY MAP Explorer 218 (Wyre Forest & Kidderminster) or Explorer 219 (Wolverhampton & Dudley)

A Carry on below the cliff, again ignoring paths off to the right. Farther on, by some fence posts, turn left onto a path that climbs through the trees, soon reaching the top of the edge by a small picnic area.

The fort on Kinver Edge was built 2,500 years ago during the Iron Age. Almost sheer cliff faces provided a natural defence on two sides, while the other two flanks were protected by a mighty earthwork, a high embankment overlooking a deep ditch. The scale of the undertaking remains impressive today, even more so when you realise that erosion has lowered the earthen walls and partly filled the excavation.

B To the left, a clear path follows the crest of the escarpment, soon passing above Nanny's Rock to re-enter the National Trust's land. Keep on along the ridge, shortly reaching a triangulation pillar marking the highest spot. Not far beyond, the path passes a massive embankment and ditch, part of an extensive Iron Age fort, then emerges into open ground. A viewing station lies a little farther on.

C Walk past the orientation table and go half-right at the edge of the cliff above Kinver. The path, signed 'Holy Austin Rock', then begins to descend, sometimes quite steeply, but steps ease the way down. In a clearing below, keep left, later emerging at the bottom by the end of a track at an entrance to the rock dwellings.

D When open, you can follow a path around the caves before returning to the woodland. Otherwise, keep left over a low shoulder, dropping back through the trees towards the car park, a little farther around.

? *What are the two farthest places marked on the viewing table?*

Rock houses at Kinver Edge

The Clent Hills

START Foot of Walton Hill near High Harcourt Farm
DISTANCE 2½ miles (4km)
TIME 1¾ hours
PARKING Roadside car park at start
ROUTE FEATURES Woodland and heath paths, sustained climbs

2

Although barely a stone's throw from the West Midlands conurbation, the Clent Hills could be miles from anywhere. Rising to over 1,000 ft (300m) above sea level, they offer a spectacular view across the surrounding countryside. This short walk links the two main summits, the climb onto each much less arduous than the map might suggest.

Go to the woodland behind the parking area, but instead of tackling the direct ascent ahead, bear right along a track that rises more easily along the hillside. Emerging to meet a track along the ridge, follow it up to a triangulation pillar, a short way to the right.

Ⓐ Where the path forks just beyond, keep right along the ridge, waymarked 'North Worcestershire Path'. Undulating gently downwards, continue ahead at a second marker, shortly dropping more steeply back into trees.

Climbing onto Walton Hill

PUBLIC TRANSPORT None
REFRESHMENTS Picnic tables by car park, Vine Inn at bottom of St Kenelm's Pass (children's menu) and tea bar at Visitor Centre (½ mile/800m)
PUBLIC TOILETS At Visitor Centre
ORDNANCE SURVEY MAP Explorer 219 (Wolverhampton & Dudley)

The Four Stones

Lower down, at another marker, turn off sharp right, the path doubling back down the slope. On reaching a track at the bottom beside Clee View Cottage, turn left and descend past more houses to emerge onto a lane at the bottom of St Kenelm's Pass.

B The Vine Inn lies just left, but the onward route follows a footpath directly opposite, which bends left behind the pub. Branch right at a fork by a National Trust sign, and then keep ahead at the next junction. Rounding the spur brings you to another junction; there go right to ascend the ridge. Ignore crossing paths as you gain height, eventually reaching a stile onto the open hilltop. Continue ahead, making for the obvious high point, where, beside the main path, are four standing stones and a nearby viewing table.

The panorama from the top of either hill is more than worth the climb, on a clear day revealing the Cotswolds, Malverns, Welsh hills and the Midland plateau. The **standing stones** are not of prehistoric origin but were erected at the beginning of the 18th century to create an eye-catching feature by Lord Littleton of nearby **Hagley Hall**, using stone from the same quarries that furnished the building of the hall.

C Walk on, passing them on your right, the way then joined by a path from the left. Just beyond, at a junction in a dip, bear right on a bridleway, marked 'North Worcestershire Path'. After gently losing height around the shoulder of the hill, it then drops more purposefully into trees. Keep ahead, later joining a track which emerges onto a lane at the head of St Kenelm's Pass.

D Go left to a junction. St Kenelm's Church lies ahead, about ¼ mile (400m) away, but the way back is to the right.

From the viewing table on the second hill, can you identify the first hill you climbed?

Now standing in isolation, **St Kenelm's Church** was once surrounded by a village. Built on the traditional site of Kenelm's martyrdom and by a holy well reputed to have healing powers, it was, until the Reformation, a popular place of pilgrimage. However, such practices were not encouraged under the new Order and, without the trade of the pilgrims, the community dispersed. Parts of the church are Saxon, and the finely carved doorway is Norman with the porch appearing during Tudor times. The design of the south window is attributed to the pre-Raphaelite artist, **Sir Edward Burne-Jones**.

3 *Along the River Severn to Bewdley*

START Blackstone Meadows Country Park
DISTANCE 2½ miles (4km)
TIME 1½ hours
PARKING Car park at Blackstone Meadows Country Park
ROUTE FEATURES Riverside and field paths, short walk through town centre

Just south of the ancient town of Bewdley, the River Severn is forced aside by the massive cliffs of Blackstone Rock. Below, on the opposite bank, is an attractive picnic and play area from which a riverside path meanders upstream to the town. The walk returns across pleasant rolling hills to the west, passing the historic church of St Leonard.

From the back of the car park, walk down to the Severn and follow a path, which winds through the trees along its bank into Bewdley. Approaching the town, keep to the waterfront until you reach a bridge across the river.

Ⓐ Follow the main street up into the town. Part way along on the left, housed in what used to be a butchers' shambles and abattoir, and later the fire station, is the town's museum. Also worth looking at is St Anne's Church, which stands a little farther along in the centre of the street. Approaching the church, pass it on the left and then turn left into High Street.

Ⓑ Towards the far end of the town, where the street narrows and begins to dip, are almshouses, a large white building on the right built in 1693. Turn right immediately past it along a narrow passage, signed 'Worcestershire Way' and to the Old Pals' Shelter. Behind the houses, bear left to join another path from the right and walk on over a plank bridge to

PUBLIC TRANSPORT Bus and rail (Severn Valley Railway) services to Bewdley (alternative start)
REFRESHMENTS Picnic tables at Blackstone Meadows, choice of pubs and cafés in Bewdley
PUBLIC TOILETS In Bewdley
ORDNANCE SURVEY MAP Explorer 218 (Wyre Forest & Kidderminster)

Granted a charter by Edward IV in 1472, **Bewdley** was once a busy port. Flat-bottomed barges traded with the seaport at Bristol, exchanging exotic goods from the East for local produce such as leather, corn, coal and timber. The cargoes were handled on the riverside quay, fronted by elegant Georgian buildings, an indication of the wealth amassed by the town's merchants. The graceful bridge spanning the river was designed by **Thomas Telford** and completed in 1798.

enter a meadow above a small lake. Wander ahead up an open valley, shortly joining a track, which continues rising, eventually to end at a lane.

C Cross to another track opposite and follow that down, bearing left at a fork to go beneath the bypass. The descent continues, shortly reaching some cottages by St Leonard's Church. At a junction beyond the cottages, turn left and walk out to a lane. Turn left again, but where it then bends, leave on the right to regain the riverbank and follow it upstream back to Blackstone Country Park.

Although considerably rebuilt following a lightning strike in 1877, the most ancient parts of **St Leonard's Church** date from the beginning of the 12th century. It has many interesting features, including the timbered bell-turret, which contains what is thought to be the oldest bell in the country. Also striking is the 17th-century entrance porch, sheltering a wonderfully carved doorway and part of the original Norman building. Inside, an arcade of oak columns, unique in Worcestershire, separates the south aisle from the nave.

Where in St Leonard's Church can you find a pig playing bagpipes?

Across the Severn from Bewdley's old quay

Earlswood Lakes

START Malthouse Lane

DISTANCE 2½ miles (4km)

TIME 1¼ hours

PARKING Car park off Malthouse Lane, north-east of The Lakes' station

ROUTE FEATURES Woodland paths, which may be muddy after rain

4

The group of 19th-century reservoirs at Earlswood and the old, established woodlands that lie beside them are wonderfully rich in the diversity of animal and plant life they support. While a network of meandering paths provide any number of possibilities for walks, this short, undemanding route takes you to some of the most attractive spots.

A path from the car park leads to the waterside, meeting it where an intermediate dam divides Terry's Pool from Engine Pool. Go ahead across the wooded causeway and, beyond a footbridge spanning a weir, walk left along the far bank of Terry's Pool, where you will see numerous waterbirds including coots, moorhens, swans and great crested grebe.

A On reaching a junction by a sluice, turn right over a bridge into the wood behind. Bear right at a fork, some 30 yds (27m) along and, at a crossing of paths a little farther on, again keep right, the way being marked by yellow symbols. Just before reaching a small parking area, go left to emerge over a footbridge onto the edge of an open grass field. Walk left along its length at the edge of the wood, eventually reaching a stile back into the trees at the far end, by another car park.

? *How many species of woodpecker are native to Britain?*

PUBLIC TRANSPORT Nearby bus and rail services

REFRESHMENTS Choice of nearby pubs or tearoom at craft centre

PUBLIC TOILETS None

CHILDREN'S PLAY AREA Adjacent to car park

ORDNANCE SURVEY MAP Explorer 220 (Birmingham, Walsall, Solihull & Redditch)

Earlswood Lakes

B Wander left, towards an information panel and bear right. Keep right again at a second fork a little farther on and continue descending to a footbridge. Carry on, following waymarks, eventually crossing a more open area beneath the trees. At the far side, turn left, where white symbols mark a winding path, loosely tracing the eastern boundary of the wood. Beyond a stream, the way presently reaches a bridge over the railway line.

C Instead of crossing, turn left beside the line. Soon after passing a level-crossing, the path wanders into the trees, shortly entering a small, open heath. At the far side, keep generally ahead, following the intermittently waymarked main path. Eventually, the way returns you to the bank of Terry's Pool, at the point where you first left it **A**.

New Fallings Coppice and **Clowes Wood** are at least 400 years old, and give some impression of the woodland that once extended over most of middle England. Once a valuable resource providing timber, grazing and game for the scattering of small villages that lay within them, they are now an important wildlife refuge in our modern world. Here, you will find many species of birds and a variety of trees and flowers, including the lily of the valley, which is rare in Warwickshire.

Now, turn right to continue around the head of the lake, keeping left where a path later joins. Carry on along the opposite shore, back to the dam above Engine Pool. The car park lies to the right.

Earlswood Lakes were created in the 1820s to service the nearby Stratford-upon-Avon Canal, whose 53 locks between here and the Avon, need a constant water supply. The dams and associated feeder ditches and sluices took five years to complete, and a steam pump was installed at the northern tip of **Engine Pool** to push water into the canal. By the beginning of the 20th century, the area had become a popular haunt, attracting crowds from the nearby industrial towns. On Sundays and holidays people flocked to enjoy bathing, sailing, fishing and countryside walks. So many came that the nearby station had to be built.

5 *Middle Littleton Tithe Barn*

START South Littleton
DISTANCE 2½ miles (4km)
TIME 1½ hours
PARKING Roadside parking in South Littleton
ROUTE FEATURES Undemanding field paths and tracks

A fine view to the west from Cleeve Hill and quiet countryside, where market gardening predominates, characterise this short walk to the splendid tithe barn at Middle Littleton. Unfortunately, the village pubs shown on the Ordnance Survey map have closed, but either drop to the Avon at Billington Lock or visit nearby Badsey for refreshment.

🖌 Leave the main road through South Littleton along Church Lane, which runs along the northern edge of St Michael's churchyard. Degrading to a track, it continues past houses and Church Farm to the fields beyond. Keep going past a nursery, eventually reaching the edge of the Cleeve Hill scarp.

🅐 Instead of following the track down to the River Avon, turn right through an open gateway, but then leave within a few paces, to go left through a waymarked gap. Where the path then immediately divides, branch right, passing through bushes before emerging to follow the top of the ridge north. After 350 yds (320m), look for a stile on the left. However, instead of crossing, turn through the hedge on the right. Initially following a line of century-old damson trees, walk out between the fields, continuing ahead until you eventually emerge onto a lane.

? *Why is the barn known as a 'tithe' barn?*

PUBLIC TRANSPORT Bus service to South Littleton
REFRESHMENTS Fish and chip shop in South Littleton and pub at nearby Badsey (1½ miles/2.4km), noted for its asparagus dishes
PUBLIC TOILETS None
ORDNANCE SURVEY MAP Explorer 205 (Stratford-upon-Avon & Evesham)

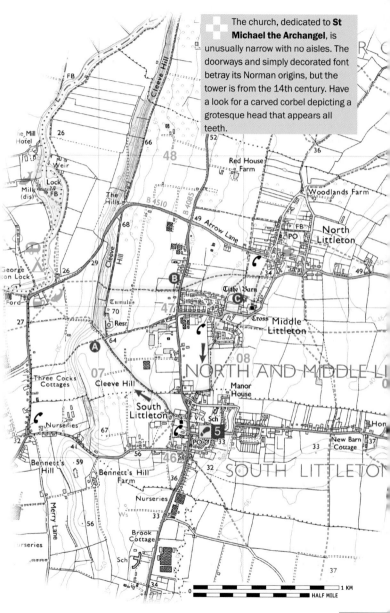

The church, dedicated to **St Michael the Archangel**, is unusually narrow with no aisles. The doorways and simply decorated font betray its Norman origins, but the tower is from the 14th century. Have a look for a carved corbel depicting a grotesque head that appears all teeth.

B Cross to a stile opposite and head left towards the far corner of the field. Continue in the same direction along an avenue of saplings to a pair of stiles. Go over the one on the right and walk ahead by the hedge to another stile. Do not cross, but instead turn right towards the back of St Nicholas' Church, leaving the field through a small garden area into the churchyard. Walk out to the lane and go right. At a left-hand bend in the village, turn right up a track and then right again to reach the tithe barn.

C Return to the road, and walk ahead to the next bend, there turning off past a play area into a small housing estate on the left. At the far end, turn right into Manor Close, and walk on through a kissing-gate into a field beyond. Follow the hedge ahead to its end, where a contained path then leads into South Littleton. Emerging at a junction of lanes, go ahead to return to the main road. ●

> Looking more like some vast ancient church than an agricultural building, **the barn** was commissioned by the Abbott of Evesham in 1376. Measuring 140 ft (42m) by 40 ft (12m), it is the largest surviving building of its type in the country and is built from the local blue Lias stone, its corners and quoins finished in harder Cotswold stone.

Middle Littleton Tithe Barn

Wilmcote and Mary Arden's House

START Wilmcote	
DISTANCE 2¾ miles (4.4km)	
APPROXIMATE TIME 1¾ hours	
PARKING Street parking in village	
ROUTE FEATURES Field paths and canal towpaths	

6

The tiny village of Wilmcote, just north-east of Stratford-upon-Avon, would perhaps have sunk into obscurity if the childhood cottage of Shakespeare's mother, Mary Arden, were not still standing. Every year it is visited by innumerable tourists, few of whom take the trouble to explore the surrounding countryside. But this easy walk does just that, returning beside the Stratford-upon-Avon Canal.

🖉 Head north-east from the village, as if to follow the lane to Aston Cantlow. However, opposite the post office and store, turn right onto a track. Continue through a gate and over a stile beside paddocks behind Mary Arden's house, eventually to emerge into the corner of a large grass field. Keep ahead, crossing more stiles at the far side into the next field, and continue with the boundary now on your left. Carry on through a gap, but before reaching the far end of the open grazing, look for a gate and stile on the left.

🅐 Do not cross, but instead turn right and walk out over the field, heading towards the ruins of Broadlow Cottage on the far side, half hidden in the trees. Pass through a gate and bear left beside the buildings. Follow the field edge around to the left to walk parallel to the canal. As you approach the far end of the field, you will see a bridge.

PUBLIC TRANSPORT Rail and bus service to Wilmcote
REFRESHMENTS Mary Arden Inn and Mason's Arms in village
PUBLIC TOILETS For visitors to Mary Arden's House
ORDNANCE SURVEY MAP Explorer 205 (Stratford-upon-Avon & Evesham)

In the grounds of Mary Arden's House

B On the opposite bank, turn right and follow the towpath back towards Wilmcote, after ¾ mile (1.2km), passing beneath a road bridge by Wilmcote Station. Keep going beside the canal for a farther 500 yds (456m) to the next bridge, Canada Bridge.

C Cross to the opposite bank and walk away, following a winding track over the fields. Emerging onto a drive, turn right, and then go right again at the top onto a lane, passing St Andrew's Church as you return to the village centre. ●

Have a look inside **St Andrew's Church**, its walls have an unusual decoration. Executed by a former vicar around the end of the 19th century, some 60 years after the church was built, it consists of biblical scenes drawn onto sheets of zinc, some of which have then been coloured in red. Notice, too, a hark-back to the customs of earlier days, when the sexes of the congregation were separated; hooks for the gentlemen's top hats are provided on the south side where they sat.

? *Canada Bridge is a modern version of the original 'roving bridge'. Why do you think it is split in the middle?*

Although the building used as the visitor entrance is often mistaken for **Mary Arden's House**, it is, in fact, the one next door in the centre of the village, which belonged to her father, Robert Arden. Mary married John Shakespeare, then a successful glover and wool dealer in Stratford-upon-Avon, in 1557 and bore him eight children. There were four boys, William being the eldest, and four daughters, three of whom did not survive infancy. Some 20 years after their marriage, John's business failed, and Mary's inherited land from her father had to be mortgaged. Yet, in the end, even this did not save her husband from bankruptcy, and he had eventually to call on William, by then a successful playwright in London, to bail him out of his insolvency.

7 *Waseley Hills Country Park*

START Waseley Hills Visitor Centre
DISTANCE 3 miles (4.8km)
TIME 2 hours
PARKING Visitor Centre car park (pay and display)
ROUTE FEATURES Field and woodland paths, sustained climb

Rising steeply to the west of Rubery are the Waseley Hills, 150 acres (60 ha) of unspoilt, rolling ground. Steep, wooded valleys, which are a haven for a wide variety of plants, insects, birds and animals, cleave the western flanks, and there is much to see at any time of year.

Leave the Visitor Centre car park through a gate to the left of the Windmill Café. Bear right, climbing the hill at the edge of open grassland. Ignore a stile, a short distance along and continue up by the fence. After passing beneath power cables, the way curves around to the left, rising to a corner by a memorial seat.

A There, go over a stile on the right to follow a stepped path that falls beside a small copse. Continue over a second stile into a grassy valley, crossing the head of a stream before accompanying it downhill into woodland. Cross more stiles on the descent through Segbourne Coppice, the path eventually meeting a track at the bottom.

B Turn left, and then keep ahead, passing through gates and across a drive. Shortly, the track curves right, dropping to Chadwich Grange Farm. Leave it on the bend, going forward over a stile into a

Grazing sheep, and more lately cattle, have kept the rounded hills of Waseley clear of trees for centuries, and indeed its name derives from the Saxon words, 'waer' meaning sheep and 'ley' meaning field.

PUBLIC TRANSPORT None
REFRESHMENTS Café at Visitor Centre
PUBLIC TOILETS At beginning of walk
CHILDREN'S PLAY AREA By start of walk
ORDNANCE SURVEY MAP Explorer 219 (Wolverhampton & Dudley)

The rich mixed woodlands cloaking the sheltered valleys and lower flanks of the hills are important wildlife habitats and support a surprising variety of plant and animal species. Go quietly and you may catch sight of a fox, or wait as dusk falls in late spring and you may be lucky enough to see badgers playing. There is certainly plenty of evidence that they abound here in the numerous burrows passed during the walk.

0   1 KM
HALF MILE

Long Saw Croft
Round Saw Croft
79
Sandhills Farm
Newtown Farm
Newtown Lane
Gannow Green Farm
FB
248
V 7 P
Gannow Green
Duck Pool Farm
78
Dayhouse
Romsleyhill Farm
Romsley Manor Farm 256
281 275
Putney Lane
261
Romsley Hill
Dayhouse Farm
260
Dayhouse Bank
219
230
Farley Farm
A
Chapman's Hill
Chapman's Hill Farm
Windmill Hill
D
Thistle Grove Farm
96
Money Lane
B
Barnes Close
Segbourne Coppice
97
Waseley Hill
Waseley Hills Country Park
219
Waseleyhill Farm
98
FB
Schools
Monarch's Way
77
Pit (dis)
Pit (dis)
178
195
Chadwich Grange Farm
Holywell Farm
Leisure Centre
North W
Resr
Square Coppice
Chadwich Manor Estate
C
Redhill Farm
Holy Well
171
Redhill Lane
Reservoir
Spring Pool
Chadwich Manor
FB
76
Chadwich Wo
Beaconwood
A 38(T)
4
Lydiate Ash
Beacon Farm
Beacon Lane
The Limes
Woodrow

long field. Carry on to its far right-hand corner, where another stile leads into a wood. Through it, bear left across a field to reach its opposite hedge.

C Now following the Monarch's Way, climb beside the boundary to the upper corner and continue along the edge of the subsequent field. Passing through a gate at the top, walk on over the grassy summit, dropping to a path on the far side above Rubery. Turn left, and through successive gates, keep ahead to pass a small plantation on the high point.

D Carry on in the same direction, passing through a gap onto Windmill Hill. Beyond the observation platform, the hill falls away towards the Visitor Centre, which then comes into view below.

> **?** *How can you tell the footprint of a fox from that of a badger?*

Gnarled tree roots beside the path

Sutton Park

8

START Bracebridge Pool car park
DISTANCE 3¼ miles (5.2km)
TIME 1½ hours
PARKING Car park above Bracebridge Pool (access from A454 at Four Oaks – charge on summer Sundays and bank holidays)
ROUTE FEATURES Woodland paths, some inclined to be muddy

Sutton Park epitomises the act of survival, a vast area of natural woodland and open heath completely surrounded by conurbation. Rich in plant and animal life, it is a wonderful place to explore throughout the year and, while there are any number of walks you might take, this one reveals some of its many secrets.

Through a barrier beyond the car park, the main track leads to Bracebridge Pool. There, bear right past the restaurant to discover a path winding through Pool Hollies above the lake. Streams draining the hillside can make the way muddy, but duckboards pave the worst patches.

Ⓐ Shortly, the path emerges into a clearing. Turn right, ascending a broad path from the water at the edge of the woodland. After some 200 yds (183m), bear left across more open heath to crest a shallow rise. Gently descending beyond,

Designated a National Nature Reserve, **Sutton Park** is one of the most important nature conservation sites in the Midlands. It once formed part of Sutton Chase, a 12th-century deer park created by Henry I for the Earls of Warwick, but following the persuasion of John Vessey, Bishop of Exeter and a native of Sutton, was granted to the town in 1528 by Henry VIII.

join a clearer track from the right to meander generally ahead, ignoring lesser paths. You are likely to see Exmoor ponies grazing the glades as the path eventually rounds the western tip of Little Bracebridge Pool.

PUBLIC TRANSPORT Bus service to Four Oaks Gate (¾ mile/1.2km)
REFRESHMENTS Restaurant and snack counter by Bracebridge Pool
PUBLIC TOILETS Nearest at Sutton Park Visitor Centre (1 mile/1.6km)
CHILDREN'S PLAY AREA Near Visitor Centre
ORDNANCE SURVEY MAP Explorer 220 (Birmingham, Walsall, Solihull & Redditch)

0 ——————————— 1 KM
HALF MILE

Streetly

Streetly Clumps

Lodge

Little Bracebridge Pool

B FB

Streetly Belt

Streetly Wood

CH

Bracebridge Pool

A

B4138

Gum Slade (Path)

Mayor's Arbour

Sch

99

B415

Druid's Well

C

09

Darnel Hurst

Pool Hollies

8 P

Druid's Well

98

Earthwork

E

FBs

FB

FB

10

B4138 ROMAN ROAD

Warden's Belt

Roman Street

Upper Nut Hurst

Blackroot Pool

Meml

152

Sutton Park

D

97

Lower Nut Hurst

FBs

Keeper's Well

Hill Hurst

Keeper's Pool

PC

FB

Holly Hurst

SUTTON COLDFI

96

Wyndle Wood

FB

La Reserve

129

Weir

Powell's Pool

CH

127

Schs

Described by a Victorian writer as 'one of the prettiest spots in England', **Bracebridge Pool** is one of seven artificial lakes within the park. They were constructed over the centuries to provide a ready source of fish as well as to pound water for several mills. The smaller pool passed on the walk was a 'fish stew', where fish could be fattened and more easily caught when required. Today, they are still well-stocked and are a favourite haunt for anglers. Some fish grow to quite a size, and the record catch was a carp, weighing in at 35lb 13oz. Look out in summer for dragonflies, which flit around the reeds at the water's edge.

Bracebridge Pool

B Beyond a stream, make for a gated bridge piercing the railway embankment in front. Emerging at a fork on the far side, take the left branch. A grassy and sometimes boggy path leads by a clump of birch and then across open heath, shortly reaching a broad track. To the right, past a parking area, it ends at a tarmac drive.

C The onward way lies to the left alongside the drive, leading to a junction some ¾ mile (1.2km) away. There, bear left and then immediately go left again, along a gravel track heading towards Nut Hurst. In the trees, follow the main path to the right, soon descending to another body of water, Blackroot Pool.

D Walk left on an undulating woodland path above its bank, ignoring minor paths until you reach an obvious crossing. There, turn right through a gateway in a broken fence and keep with a clear path down, across a marshy area and over a stream to reach a broad track beneath the railway embankment. Follow it left until you reach a bridge.

E On the other side, a rough gravel path climbs away at the edge of wooded heath, shortly returning you to the car park from which the walk began. ●

> **?** Look for a stone monument by the junction in the centre of the park. What does it commemorate?

9 *Hanbury Hall*

START Piper's Hill

DISTANCE 3½ miles (5.6km)

TIME 2 hours

PARKING Car park on B4091

ROUTE FEATURES Woodland and field paths

Rolling hills overlook the spa town of Droitwich, important since Roman times for its briny springs that bubble from the ground, ten times saltier than the waters of the Dead Sea. Roman roads and ancient salt ways criss-cross the landscape, where fine views, an interesting church and a charming country house are the highlights of this enjoyable stroll.

Although **Hanbury church** was substantially rebuilt in the late 18th century, it occupies an ancient site. British tribes had fortified the hilltop some 500 years before the Romans arrived to build their own fort and, after they left, Saxon Christians worshipped here. While it stands in isolation now, during medieval times, a village clustered around the church. Among the funerary monuments inside are those to the Vernon family, who built **Hanbury Hall**. On the north wall are the original models for the Nativity and Resurrection panels, executed by Walter Gilbert for the reredos in Liverpool's Anglican Cathedral.

A track leads from the car park through the woods to Knotts Farm. Walk past the entrance, and, where the path forks just beyond, bear left. Carry on through the trees around the foot of Piper's Hill. Where the path again splits at the far side of the wood, branch right and, emerging from the trees, join a track from the left. Follow it ahead past a hoary old oak before another farm and on through a gate into the corner of a field. Cross and keep going beyond, climbing to enter a churchyard on top of the hill.

PUBLIC TRANSPORT None

REFRESHMENTS For visitors to Hanbury Hall

PUBLIC TOILETS For visitors to Hanbury Hall

ORDNANCE SURVEY MAP Explorer 204 (Worcester & Droitwich Spar)

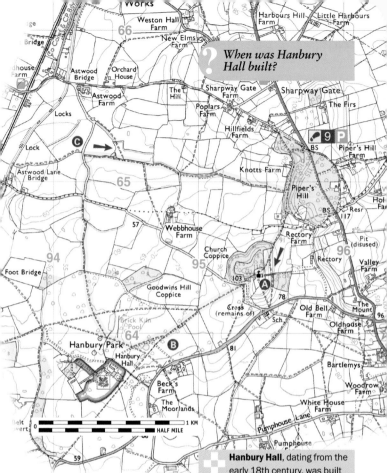

When was Hanbury Hall built?

A Walk around to the front of the church and down the lane beyond to a junction. Cross to a kissing-gate into a field opposite and head out from the corner along a grassy track. Over a stile at the far side, continue along a grassy oak avenue, eventually to emerge on a metalled drive.

Hanbury Hall, dating from the early 18th century, was built in the style of Wren and has remained remarkably unchanged over the centuries. The outstanding decoration of the hall and staircase, a status symbol of its day, was by James Thornhill and depicts the story of the Greek hero **Achilles** from Homer's *Iliad*. The gardens, too, are special, having been restored to reflect the period when the hall was built.

B *Hanbury Hall lies directly ahead, and if you wish to visit, go left and then right around a wooded pool, crossing the parkland to reach the main drive and entrance by the visitor car park.* Otherwise, continue the walk ahead along the service drive. After some 200 yds (183m), cross a stile on the right and strike away on a shallow left diagonal to another stile at the bottom. Then, bear right across the parkland beyond, heading right of the prominent transmitter masts, visible in the distance. Cross a stile beside a gate at the far side and continue ahead at the edge of fields, eventually emerging onto a lane at a junction.

C Follow the lane opposite for ¼ mile (400m) until you reach a waymarked stile by a gate on the right. Walk away along the perimeter of successive fields, keeping ahead when you reach a crossing track. Ignore a path on the left over a plank bridge, instead walk on at the field edge. However, before reaching the far end, turn through the thicket on the left where a footbridge spans the stream. Follow the right boundary away, crossing a second bridge at the next corner and on up the field beyond. Leave over a stile at the top, returning you to the woodland below Piper's Hill. Go left, retracing your steps past Knotts Farm to the car park. ●

Hanbury Hall

Cannock Chase and the German Military Cemetery

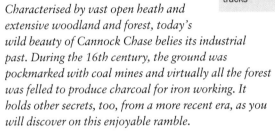

START Visitor Centre
DISTANCE 3¾ miles (6km)
TIME 2 hours
PARKING Car park by Visitor Centre (pay and display)
ROUTE FEATURES Clear heath and woodland tracks

10

Characterised by vast open heath and extensive woodland and forest, today's wild beauty of Cannock Chase belies its industrial past. During the 16th century, the ground was pockmarked with coal mines and virtually all the forest was felled to produce charcoal for iron working. It holds other secrets, too, from a more recent era, as you will discover on this enjoyable ramble.

From the Visitor Centre car park, turn right and walk up to Marquis Drive, where, on the corner, is a memorial to those who lost their lives in the Burma Campaign. Now go left, and when you reach the road carry on ahead to a crossroads.

A Cross to a footpath opposite to the right, signed 'Heart of England Way' and follow it into the forest. The waymarked route dog-legs right and then left, when it shortly meets a crossing track, doing the same again, a little farther on, before eventually ending at another road.

B A path opposite leads through more open countryside, the way falling easily between young pine trees and birch to reach a broad crossing track. Turn left and continue down into the Sherbrook Valley.

? *When was the German Military Cemetery inaugurated?*

PUBLIC TRANSPORT None
REFRESHMENTS Café, picnic tables and barbecue area at Visitor Centre
PUBLIC TOILETS Near Visitor Centre
ORDNANCE SURVEY MAP Explorer 244 (Cannock Chase)

Cannock Chase

C At another junction there, go left again, keeping to the main path at the edge of open heath. Bear left at a waymarked fork, climbing towards mature forest ahead, where a track joins from the left at Gospel Place. Go right, and keep on until you reach the entrance to the German Military Cemetery.

D Retrace your steps along the track to the edge of the cemetery and turn right onto a path running between mature trees and recent planting. When it forks, bear right and then, at a junction of paths a little farther on, keep straight ahead, shortly emerging onto a road. Cross to an opening opposite and, ignoring the track off right, keep walking in the same direction

for ⅓ mile (530m) to reach another road. Turn right on a parallel path through the trees, but where it shortly diverges from the carriageway, go out to the road, continuing to the entrance of the Brindley Village car park a little farther on.

E Turn in through the parking area and follow a track at the far side. At a junction, 50 yds (46m) on, choose the left fork, waymarked blue, and follow it around the now-wooded site once occupied by Brindley Military Hospital. Keep ahead where paths later cross, the way eventually emerging from the trees. It then loses height, winding down to join a main foresters' track.

F Some 50 yds (46m) to the left, go left, leave again on a grass track that drops into a shallow dip, where a rising gravel track then leads the way ahead. At a fork at the top of the rise, bear right, but then, just a short distance on, take the left branch and walk out to the road. Cross to a wooded heath opposite and follow a path ahead and then left to return to the Visitor Centre.

The **German Military Cemetery** is the only one in Britain and contains the remains of some 5,000 German servicemen who lost their lives on British soil during the two World Wars. More German soldiers from the Great War lie in the **Commonwealth Cemetery**, just a little farther along the road. Tragically, many of the men died while waiting to be repatriated after the war ended, not from wounds, but as the result of a terrible influenza epidemic that swept through Europe in 1918.

11 *Kenilworth Castle*

START Kenilworth
DISTANCE 4¼ miles (6.8km)
TIME 2½ hours
PARKING Car park by the castle
ROUTE FEATURES Field paths and tracks

Unlike its neighbour, Warwick, Kenilworth Castle is a ruin, but none the less imposing. There is a splendid view from the valley behind, where the walk leads past an intriguing earthwork, all that remains of a royal pleasure palace. For a longer day-out, you can easily extend the route to nearby Honiley, where stands a splendid early 18th-century church.

Approach the castle from the south (by its main car park) and bear left below the elevated causeway, which leads to the main gate. Through a kissing-gate, follow the base of the castle wall around two sides to its north-west corner. There, walk ahead to leave the open field by a gate beside a pink thatched cottage.

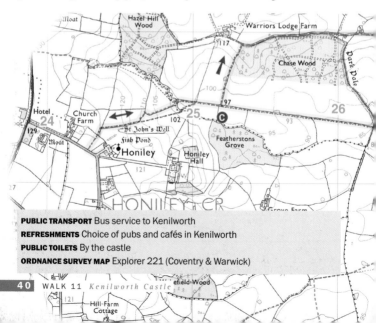

PUBLIC TRANSPORT Bus service to Kenilworth
REFRESHMENTS Choice of pubs and cafés in Kenilworth
PUBLIC TOILETS By the castle
ORDNANCE SURVEY MAP Explorer 221 (Coventry & Warwick)

A Turn left onto a gently rising track and walk away from the castle. Where the track splits at High House Farm, take the right fork past the cottage, which eventually leads out to a broad crossing track. Continue ahead over the meadow beyond, bearing left to pass grassy mounds and ditches that mark the outline of The Pleasance.

B At the far side, cross a second track to a stile opposite and carry on ahead with the hedge on your left. Keep going over a second stile to cross a ditch, Park Dale, an ancient boundary marking the edge of the Honiley estate. Carry on at the edge of the fields beyond, until eventually you reach a crossing track.

> Encompassing the popular ideal of everything an English castle should be and steeped in centuries of intrigue and romance, the ruin was the inspiration for one of **Sir Walter Scott's** best known historical novels, *Kenilworth*, written in 1821.

> **Which queen is depicted on the inn sign opposite Kenilworth Castle's northern entrance?**

C *To extend the walk to Honiley, ½ mile away (800m), follow the continuing waymarked track ahead over the fields.* Otherwise, turn right up the track, climbing past Chase Wood to meet another track near Warriors Lodge Farm. There, turn right and walk back beside the top edge of the wood. When the trees finish, keep going past Pleasance Farm to a group of cottages farther on where you will find a waymarked stile on the right.

D Walk downfield on a left diagonal, heading towards the castle. Over a stile in the middle, continue to the far-bottom corner. Cross to the next field, turn left and go through a copse into the adjacent enclosure. Resume your heading towards the castle across the ensuing fields, eventually meeting the track along which you began the walk. When you reach the pink cottage, however, keep ahead to emerge onto a road by the old village. Turn right and walk past the castle's northern gate, where you will find a path skirting its eastern flanks that leads back to the start point. ●

Founded in the early 12th century by Geoffrey de Clinton, the **castle** soon passed into the hands of the kings of England, who successively strengthened its defences over the next century to help protect the often-insecure tenure of their thrones. It was later granted to the de Montforts, who fortified the castle against the crown during the Barons' War in 1266, but the garrison succumbed to disease and starvation after a **nine-month siege**. The castle's colourful history continued until the end of the Civil War, when Cromwell had it partly demolished and it fell into ruin.

Kenilworth Castle

Shugborough

START Milford Common
DISTANCE 4½ miles
(7.2km)
TIME 2½ hours
PARKING Car park on
Milford Common (pay
and display)
ROUTE FEATURES
Woodland and field
tracks and paths, canal
towpath

*At the northern tip of Cannock Chase, the
rolling heath abruptly ends as the land
falls into the flat, meandering valleys of
the Penk and Trent. This walk contrasts
the tree-covered hills with the farmland
beyond and gives an opportunity to visit
Shugborough Park Farm and Hall, the
seat of the Earls of Lichfield.*

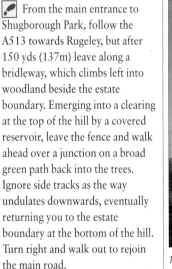 From the main entrance to
Shugborough Park, follow the
A513 towards Rugeley, but after
150 yds (137m) leave along a
bridleway, which climbs left into
woodland beside the estate
boundary. Emerging into a clearing
at the top of the hill by a covered
reservoir, leave the fence and walk
ahead over a junction on a broad
green path back into the trees.
Ignore side tracks as the way
undulates downwards, eventually
returning you to the estate
boundary at the bottom of the hill.
Turn right and walk out to rejoin
the main road.

Tower of the Winds

PUBLIC TRANSPORT Bus service to Milford
REFRESHMENTS Picnic tables, the Barley Mow pub and the Little Fawn Café
by Milford Common. Tearooms at Shugborough and a riverside café at Great
Haywood.
ADVENTURE PLAYGROUND At Shugborough Park Farm
PUBLIC TOILETS Opposite green at Milford Common, and for visitors at
Shugborough
ORDNANCE SURVEY MAP Explorer 244 (Cannock Chase)

Miller's workshop at Shugborough Park Farm

C When you reach the junction with the Staffordshire and Worcestershire Canal, turn left beneath the bridge and follow its towpath past a marina. Just beyond, an aqueduct takes the canal over the River Trent. After Swivel Bridge, the canal broadens into reed-filled pools, and below the high ground to the north-west is the ornate Tixall Gatehouse. Keep going beyond Oldhill Bridge and Tixall Lock, eventually to reach Tixall Bridge.

A Follow it left, shortly passing a service entrance to Shugborough. Two hundred yards (183m) farther on, take a woodland path, signed 'Great Haywood'. Beyond a stream is an estate road, which, to the right, leads across the park to the farm and hall. Later on at successive forks, bear right and then left to pass Park Farm.

B *At the next fork, to visit the hall, go left*, but otherwise, bear right, shortly reaching the 16th-century Essex Bridge spanning the confluence of the rivers Trent and Penk. Just beyond, there is a second bridge over the Trent and Mersey Canal, however, instead of crossing, bear right to join the towpath and then go left beneath the bridge.

D Leave the towpath immediately beyond it and climb onto the lane above. Turn right and walk away from the canal, soon returning to Milford.

Viscount Anson took a keen interest in agricultural development and commissioned Samuel Wyatt to design **Park Farm** around 1800. Not only did it allow him to try out the improved farming ideas of the day, but produced supplies and an income for the estate. The farmhouse itself is furnished to depict how it may have looked at the beginning of the 19th century, and in the outbuildings are displays showing different aspects of farm work. The mill is particularly interesting and contains a workshop where all manner of repairs were undertaken.

The **Trent and Mersey Canal** was opened in 1777. Running for 93 miles (150km) between Preston Brook and Derwent Mouth, it connected with nine other canals. This junction with the Staffordshire and Worcestershire provided a link with the River Severn at Stourport, 46 miles (74km) away, and came into operation in 1772. Despite competition from other Midland canals, and later the railways, both canals carried regular trade until the beginning of the 20th century. Today they are again busy, but with leisure boats replacing the cargo barges.

> **?** *How many arches are there supporting Essex Bridge?*

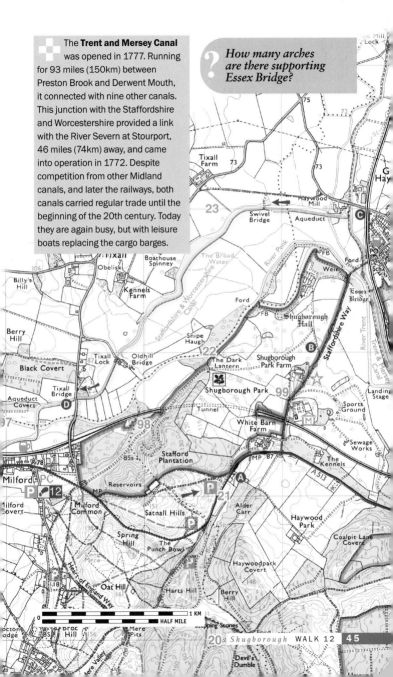

13 Alrewas to Fradley Junction

Described as one of the most picturesque canal-side locations in the Midlands, Fradley Junction marks the point where the Coventry and Trent and Mersey Canals meet. This walk from the pleasant old town of Alrewas follows a stretch of each of the canals, passing several locks along the way, where a passing boat will always provide some interest.

START Alrewas
DISTANCE 4¾ miles (7.6km)
TIME 2¾ hours
PARKING Roadside parking in Alrewas
ROUTE FEATURES Canal towpaths, lanes and field paths

Follow Main Street out of the town, but immediately after crossing the Trent and Mersey Canal at Kent's Bridge, drop left to the towpath and walk away. Not far along is an accommodation bridge, hard up against which, on its opposite side, is Bagnall Lock, the first passed on this walk. Beyond a modern road bridge, the canal continues between fields, passing Common Lock and, later, Hunt's Lock. Although it is not far to Fradley Junction, which lies beyond a bridge a little farther on,

there are two more locks to pass. The buildings between them on the left were built as a maintenance depot and over to the right is a small reservoir that supplies the canal.

The Swan opposite Fradley Junction quickly became an important stopping place along the canal and, in addition to meeting the needs of the bargees, maintenance workers, officials and boat passengers, provided extensive stabling to cater for the horses that hauled the barges along.

PUBLIC TRANSPORT Bus service to Alrewas
REFRESHMENTS Choice of pubs in Alrewas and the Swan at Fradley Junction
PUBLIC TOILETS None
CHILDREN'S PLAY AREA Beside route at Alrewas
ORDNANCE SURVEY MAP Explorer 245 (The National Forest, Burton upon Trent & Swadlincote)

From the Swan Inn, retrace your steps along the canal back to the last bridge and cross to the opposite bank. *To answer the question, you must first go to the maintenance yard, and then return along the same bank to the junction, there turning left onto the Coventry Canal, a waterway signpost boldly pointing the way to that city.* Follow the towpath for 1¼ miles (2km), passing beneath New Bridge and later, a modern road bridge, to reach Fradley Bridge (number 90).

The **Trent and Mersey Canal** was fully operative by 1777, providing the Potteries manufacturers, led by **Josiah Wedgwood**, with an effective means of distributing their wares. This was followed later by the **Coventry Canal**, initially intended to provide an outlet for the coalfields north of Coventry. Considerably delayed, having overspent its original budget, it was not completed until 1790. Part of the rapidly expanding network of canals that radiated from Birmingham, they continued to serve the Midlands industries into the 20th century, despite competition from the railways.

Fradley Junction

B Immediately beyond it, leave the canal bank, climbing up to the lane above and turn right. At the end, opposite Fradley School, walk right, but then, just after a small brick-built church, go left into Old Hall Lane. Follow that, past the farm that gave it its name, and continue around the right-hand bend at the top to a crossroads.

C Turn left into Long Lane. After 80 yds (73m), turn into the first field on the right and cut diagonally across to a stile. Continue to the far corner where you will emerge onto a track beside Moo Moo Cottage. Go right, but leave again a few paces along into the corner of the left-hand field and follow its edge away, crossing a plank bridge to the field beyond. There bear right, heading for a kissing-gate to carry on in the same direction, finally emerging onto Daisy Lane.

D To the right, the lane leads out to a busy main road. Cross to a

> **?** *Where and by who was the canal-side crane made?*

The ancient settlement of **Alrewas** grew beside the Tame, which nourished its eel and basket industries. Sixteenth-century houses still line the main street and its fine parish church, well worth visiting, has a history from at least the 9th century.

cycle path opposite and then turn left, following a short residential street around to a car park by a large sports field. Walk ahead at its edge, passing a children's play area to emerge onto a track through an opening in a hedge at its far end. Continue along a narrow alleyway directly opposite, which leads back to Main Street in Alrewas. ●

Farm
Lodge
Chimney
MP 58
Gas Compressor Station
Overley
FB
W
1 KM
0   HALF MILE

Alrewas
13
Manor Farm
Bagnall Lock
MS

Pyford Brook
15
Trent & Mersey Canal

Common Lock
16
Bagnall
Daisy Lane
D
58
56
Long Lane
Fox Lane

Towing Path
15
58
Blackheath

Hunt's Lock
Keeper's Lock
Sale Lane
The Sale Farm
W
09
ndyhill
Sale Pit
The Sale
14
ALREWAS AND FRADLEY CP
58

New Bridge
62
Old Hall Farm
C
PO
Crown Inns Farm

Coventry Canal
62 Hay End Road
School
Fradley
MS
Rc

Fradley Bridge
Ryecroft

Airfield (disused)
B
13

Common Lane

66 MP

East
Business Park
Meml
12 Hilliard

At **Bagnall Lock** notice how the lock gate arms are cranked to allow them to operate in close proximity to the bridge, a feature much evident along this section. Outside the **Old Boat** pub, over to the right, stands a stationary **steam engine**. These were commonly moved around farms to provide power for a whole range of agricultural equipment, from wood saws to threshing machines. They were even used for ploughing, with engines stationed at opposite sides of the field dragging a plough back and forth on cables between them.

14 *Henley-in-Arden*

START Henley-in-Arden
DISTANCE 4½ miles (7.2km)
TIME 3 hours
PARKING Various locations in town
ROUTE FEATURES Field and meadow paths

Beginning in Henley, one of Warwickshire's most attractive towns, the walk heads north-east, following the former Henley-in-Arden Railway. Returning along the Heart of England Way, it leads over the hilltop site of Beaudesert Castle from where, on a fine day, there is a view to the Malvern Hills. The castle was built in the 11th century on the site of an early British hill fort.

Leave Henley beside St John the Baptist's Church, along Beaudesert Lane. At the end, just past St Nicholas' Church, a kissing-gate opens onto the hillside below Beaudesert Mount. Through a second gate on the left, cross the churchyard and a clump of trees to a meadow and continue to a bridge across a stream on the left. Head for the far-right corner of the field beyond, where a contained path follows another stream. At the end, go left along a track to the main road.

Ⓐ Turn right, but some 20 yds (18m) beyond the buttresses of a now-dismantled bridge that once carried the Henley-in-Arden Railway, leave over a waymarked stile on the right. Through trees and over a bridge, the way enters a field. Cross to a stile in the middle of the far boundary and continue across the subsequent field to its far left-hand corner. Over a stile, walk right up a narrow enclosure past Whitehall Farm to join a track at the top. Continue to its end and go left.

PUBLIC TRANSPORT Bus and rail services to Henley-in-Arden
REFRESHMENTS Choice of cafés, pubs and an ice cream parlour in Henley-in-Arden
PUBLIC TOILETS In Henley-in-Arden
ORDNANCE SURVEY MAP Explorer 220 (Birmingham, Walsall, Solihull & Redditch)

With only a little over 200 yds (183m) separating them, it is claimed that **St John's** and **St Nicholas'** are the two closest parish churches in the country. St Nicholas' is the oldest, the site possibly being Saxon, and has bold Norman decorative carving in the form of dog-tooth patterning around the doorway and chancel arch.

B Beyond the gateway to Buckley Farm, follow a track on the right past a house and then turn left before a barn to a kissing-gate. Behind the barn and past another house, carry on uphill in a meadow to a wood. Over a stile, continue through the trees and then straight across the next field, passing left of a copse at its far side.

C Through a gap, watch for a hidden ditch on the left as you walk forward to follow the hedge.

Reaching the next corner, wind through a gap on the right and then left through a second opening, to carry on ahead, joining the right-hand hedge. At a junction at the far end of the field, the right of way continues along the track opposite, around the perimeter of Ireland's Farm. Immediately beyond a barn on your right, it then passes through a gap into the field on the left and follows the edge of cultivation to the top of the hill. Emerging onto a track, turn right and walk back to Ireland's Farm.

D Just before the farmyard, go left through a gateway onto a descending grass track. Eventually entering a narrow field, cross to a gated bridge at the far side. Carry on up by a fence to a track at the top near Coppice Corner Farm, which leads over a bridge spanning the disused railway. Follow it down to Henley Road.

E Turn right but, immediately over a bridge, go right again on a track to Holly Bank Farm. As you pass into the second field, leave to climb beside its left-hand hedge. Bearing left over a stile at the top, keep on up the hill, crossing successive fields before reaching a track by Hungerford Farm. Cross

and continue in the same direction towards a strip of woodland ahead.

F Follow a path left through the trees to leave by a stile on the right, about 120 yds (109m) along. Head across to the far-left corner of the field, and there follow a track left above a grassy escarpment. Shortly, the way falls along the slope. Keep ahead in the dip to ascend Beaudesert Mount, dropping at the far side back to St Nicholas' Church. ●

> *Have a look at the Millennium Window in St John the Baptist's Church. What village trades are represented?*

St Nicholas' Church below Beaudesert Mount

Sambourne to Coughton Court

An elegant mansion, steeped in the history of Catholic revolts and the Gunpowder Plot and with secret passages and priest holes, makes an exciting objective for this excellent countryside ramble. Beginning from the tiny Warwickshire village of Sambourne, it wanders through gentle farmland to the River Arrow before returning by a roundabout route.

START Sambourne

DISTANCE 4½ miles (7.2km)

TIME 3 hours

PARKING Roadside parking in Sambourne

ROUTE FEATURES Undemanding field paths and tracks

15

A track leaves the village green beside a shelter on its eastern side, leading over stiles into a field. Carry on to the far-left corner and continue at the edge of the next field to pass Sambourne Hall Farm. Beyond, a track takes the way past an isolated barn and on across the fields.

Ⓐ At the bottom, go over a stile and bear left to follow a hedge on your right along the lower field. At the far corner, cross another stile over to the left and continue across the fields, still with the hedge on

Be careful where you park in the village, for the motor car has caused contention there for almost 70 years. As far back as the 1930s, residents complained about rubbish and parked cars marring the village green, a problem exacerbated by a weekly stock market. Eventually **a bylaw** was passed **prohibiting parking and litter**, and although strong protests followed, it was vigorously enforced and still operates today.

your right. Eventually, the way leads naturally to run beside a stream on your left. Follow it, ignoring a bridge and soon leaving

PUBLIC TRANSPORT Bus service to Sambourne

REFRESHMENTS Pubs in Sambourne and Coughton and tearoom at Coughton Court

PUBLIC TOILETS For visitors to Coughton Court

ORDNANCE SURVEY MAP Explorer 220 (Birmingham, Walsall, Solihull & Redditch)

the fields onto a main road, the A435, beside Cain Bridge.

B The old Roman highway known as Ryknild Street is now a busy road, *so be careful crossing*. Then, either walk right to the entrance to Coughton Court, or, to continue the walk, go along a track opposite to the left, past a couple of estate cottages. In the meadow beyond, head out to its far-left corner. Over a couple of stiles, go left along the edge of a crop field to a track at its far end and follow that right to a stile into the next field.

C Walk out from the corner, aiming left of some barns, seen in the distance. Over stiles at the far side, continue by the River Arrow to a bridge and cross. Now, bear left, heading towards a house by Spernall Church. Emerging from the field, go left to a lane and there turn left again to re-cross the Arrow.

D The lane eventually leads back to the main road. Cross to a track opposite and follow that down, past a house and ahead at a junction to reach a field. Keep ahead along its edge, passing through a gap at its far end into the next field.

Near Sambourne Hall Farm

The Throckmortons began **Coughton Court** in the early 16th century and have lived there ever since. A staunchly Catholic family, they and their property suffered much in the centuries following the Reformation. Family involvement in a plot to remove Elizabeth in favour of **Mary Queen of Scots** and the use of the house by conspirators in the **Gunpowder Plot** provide a colourful background to one of the most attractive mansions in the area.

E At the top turn left and walk away, initially beside a hedge on the right and keeping ahead where that ends. A bridge provides access to the next field, where the way continues across to a leylandii hedge. Ignore the gate ahead and instead, go to a stile a short way to the right. Over that, walk through an enclosure behind a large house and then carry on across the field beyond to a gate opposite. Walk on to reach a stile on the right, over which, retrace your outward steps to the village green.

●

Coughton's magnificent gatehouse stands almost like a castle in its own right. How many towers does it have?

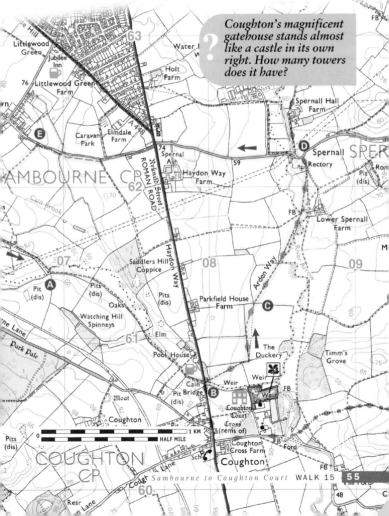

16 *Great Alne*

START Great Alne
DISTANCE 4½ miles (7.2km)
TIME 2½ hours
PARKING Lay-by beside road bridge, south-east of Great Alne
ROUTE FEATURES Mainly field paths, but with a short stretch along a sometimes-busy lane

Above the old Roman town of Alcester, the Alne twists and turns in every conceivable direction, as if trying to avoid becoming lost in the River Arrow. In earlier times, its waters powered several mills, two of which are passed on this delightful stroll through the rolling Warwickshire countryside.

Cross the River Alne towards the village, turning just beyond the bridge into a small meadow on the right. A track at the far end follows the old bed of the Alcester Railway beside the water before turning out to a lane. Some 50 yds (46m) to the right, leave through a gate beside a small structure. Cross to a stile in the far-right corner and carry on in roughly the same direction across subsequent fields, eventually leaving over a final stile onto a track.

? *Look for a sundial outside St Mary's Church. When was it erected?*

A Turn right towards the former Great Alne Mills, now converted into houses. Where the track bends left, go ahead at the side of a gate and then turn right by the mill's outflow to find a footbridge across. Walk ahead beside the river to a waymark and then go left, skirting an ornamental pond and the mill towards a tennis court. Carry on into a field behind, where a grass path leads half-right to a bridge on the far side. Cross to a lane.

B Go left and, almost immediately, right through a small gate. The way continues ahead at

PUBLIC TRANSPORT Bus service to Great Alne
REFRESHMENTS Mother Huff Cap pub with children's play area in village
PUBLIC TOILETS None
ORDNANCE SURVEY MAP Explorer 205 (Stratford-upon-Avon & Evesham)

the edge of successive fields to Walcote, finally leading out onto a lane beside the old vicarage. A path opposite then heads up to St Mary's Church on top of the hill.

C Leave the churchyard at the far side, but instead of following the path to Upton, bear off left across the grass to a stile in the bottom fence. Continue to a gate and on through a second gate to emerge on a track. Follow it to the right, passing several cottages before reaching a lane near the entrance to Manor Farm.

D Walk straight on out of the village, the lane rising to a bend. Abandon it there to go ahead into

Although a plain building with a conical tiled roof, the **dovecote** has an elaborate ogive arch above its tiny door. Built in the 14th century, just before the Black Death ravaged the country, it provided the moated grange, which once stood nearby and belonged to Evesham Abbey, with meat during the winter months. Inside are some 600 nesting boxes, which could be accessed by an ingenious revolving ladder, called a potence.

the corner of a field, and on beside the boundary over the hill. However, keep your eye open for waymarks, for the route alternates from one side of the hedge to the other three times before eventually emerging onto Trench Lane at the bottom.

Inside Haselor church

E Although the road is sometimes busy, a wide verge accompanies it for most of the way down the hill. At a junction, go ahead along a quiet lane, signed to Hoo Mill. However, at a bend before reaching the mill, walk straight on, dropping to a bridge across the River Alne. Continue across the large meadow on the other side to a gate and stile in its far-right corner and on up a track by Glebe Farm. After bending right, keep ahead in front of the farm to pass Kinwarton church and then walk on to Kinwarton Dovecote in the field beyond (the key for the dovecote can be obtained from Glebe Farm).

F Walk on past the dovecote at the head of a pond (the remnant of an ancient moat) and continue across the fields, shortly passing through a gate beside a branch of the river. There, rejoin the course of the Alcester Railway through a gate on the right and follow its raised, wooded embankment back to Great Alne. Meeting the road opposite the former station buildings, turn right to return to the lay-by. ●

Kinwarton Dovecote

Haselor, meaning hazel-covered hill, is an ancient religious site and a vague circular depression around the hill is claimed to be a **Druid circle**. The tower is Norman, but the body of the church has been much altered over the centuries. Inside, a recess in the north wall was built as a mortuary chapel, a resting place for the dead while they awaited burial. One of the walled-up openings was the '**Devil's door**', through which the banished evil could escape during a baptism.

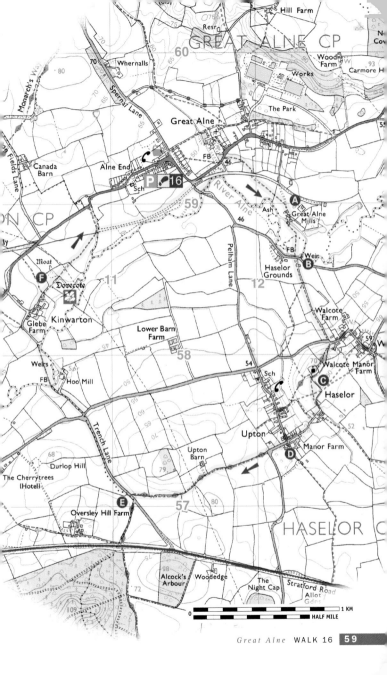

17 *Dudmaston*

START Hampton Loade
DISTANCE 5¼ miles (8.4km)
TIME 3 hours
PARKING National Trust car park (charge)
ROUTE FEATURES Riverside, woodland and field paths

For a perfect day out, travel from either Bridgnorth or Kidderminster along the Severn Valley Railway to begin this delightful walk. After following the riverbank, it meanders around the park and ornamental woodland surrounding Dudmaston Hall, where you can explore the house and its beautiful gardens before returning to the ferry at Hampton Loade to catch the train home.

From the car park, follow the field edge upstream beside the Severn, bypassing a water pumping station and pipeline bridge a little way along. Later, over a stile, the way passes into a wood. Keep going above the river until the path eventually turns away to follow a side stream. After crossing by a bridge higher up, the way emerges into a field and climbs at the edge of trees to a stile at Rookery Cottage.

A Past the cottage, walk around to the left. Join a track that continues at the edge of open parkland to Lodge Farm, and offers fine views across Dudmaston Big Pool to the house perched above its far bank. At the farm, follow the track to the right, eventually reaching the A442.

B Turn right, but after 20 yds (18m) go left at a National Trust waymark. A narrow woodland path leads to a broad grass track, which to the left heads into the forest. At a junction, some 200 yds (183m) along, take the path on the right, but shortly at a second junction, after a left-hand bend, go

PUBLIC TRANSPORT Severn Valley Railway operates a seasonal service to Hampton, where a ferry crossing connects to the start of the walk
REFRESHMENTS River and Rail pub at Hampton Loade and tearoom at Dudmaston Hall
PUBLIC TOILETS Dudmaston Hall for visitors
ORDNANCE SURVEY MAP Explorer 218 (Wyre Forest & Kidderminster)

Dudmaston Hall

right. Walk down to a clearing and turn right towards Brim Pool, there following a path to the left along its bank. Keep going at the edge of Comer Wood past Seggy Pool and on to a junction at the top end of Wall Pool.

C Now, turn off around the head of the lake and follow a path back down on the opposite bank. Emerging from the trees, part way along, turn left and keep with the field edge uphill. At the top corner, follow the hedge around a small wood-yard and continue in the field beside a lane. Eventually leave at the next corner, where the lane meets the main road.

D Cross the main road to a lodge at the entrance to Dudmaston Hall and follow the drive towards the house. *When you reach a fork, to visit the house, bear right.* Otherwise, turn left off the drive, heading towards a wood. However, at a waymark part way across the field, go right, walking parallel to the trees to a gate. Beyond, join a track, which winds down through a gate into the wood, dropping to the bottom of the valley, where it crosses a stream.

The **Hampton Loade Ferry** is the last of its kind to survive in this country, a shallow boat tethered to a fixed cable suspended between the two banks of the River Severn. It is moved by working the rudder to keep the bow into the current, which then pushes the boat across. For the past 50 years, it has been operated by two sisters and, if there is nobody about when you want to cross, just ring a bell by the water's edge.

What is the evergreen shrub rampant in the woodland around Brim Pool?

Map labels:
Heath Farm
Mose
Big Mose Farm
Sheep Wash
Comer Wood
Brim Pool
Little Holt
Dudmaston Hall
Dudmaston Big Pool
Lodge Farm
Rookery Cottage
Terns Cottages
The Holt
QUATT MALVERN C
Quatt Bridge
Dower Ho
Old Hall
The Dingle
Spring Coppice
Park Farm
New House Farm
Severn Valley Railway
River Severn
Long Covert
Millfields
Severn Way
Works
Ferry P
Lye Hall
Upper Hampton Farm
Hampton
Hampton House
Hampton Loade
Hill House
Underhill Coppice
1 KM
HALF MILE

E Climb away on the far bank, joining a track to bear right at the top. Carry on, the way shortly leading through a clearing. At the far side of the glade, before the path ahead drops steeply back into the valley, turn sharp left along a grassy track. Where that then divides, just before an open field, bear right and steadily lose height along the wooded valley-side above the Severn. Eventually, after a path drops from the left, bear right at a fork. Over a stile at the bottom, leave the wood and cross the field beyond to regain the riverbank near the pumping station and bridge. Walk downstream back to the car park. ●

Dudmaston Hall, the home of the Wolryche family who acquired the estate in 1403, was completed in the early 18th century. The hall, which passed to the National Trust in 1978, is noted for its intimate family rooms, and in them are displayed some fine furniture, paintings and sculpture, including Dutch flower paintings, topographical watercolours and modern art. **The gardens**, too, are a delight, with many flowering shrubs and fruit trees, including mulberry.

Spring daffodils in Dudmaston's gardens

18 Baddesley Clinton

There are many grand manor houses and stately homes in the Midlands, but Baddesley Clinton, surrounded by a moat and with an ancient church for company, is surely one of the prettiest. But first, this walk takes you along the Grand Union Canal, which until 1895 was known as the Warwick and Birmingham Canal.

START Kingswood Junction

DISTANCE 5¼ miles (8.4km)

TIME 3 hours

PARKING Car park at start of walk

ROUTE FEATURES Mainly canal towpaths and field paths, which may be muddy after rain

The **church** was built in the 13th century, but was considerably extended some 200 years later by **Nicholas Brome**, whose family held the manor before it passed to the **Ferrers**. It is said that his lavish generosity to the church was in expiation of his guilt for killing a priest, whom he discovered 'in his plor chockinge his wife under ye chinne'. Brome requested that after his death he be interred upright beneath the doorway, so that 'people may tread upon mee when they come into the Church'. The church was originally dedicated to St James, but changed to St Michael following its restoration in 1872.

The canal by the car park is actually the Stratford-upon-Avon. Turn right along it to the first bridge, cross to the island at the centre of the junction and bear left past a lock. Cross another bridge and follow a short linking canal beneath a railway bridge to the Grand Union.

Ⓐ Head right along the towpath. *If you want somewhere to eat, try the Tom o' the Wood on the opposite bank at the second bridge.* Otherwise, carry on along the

PUBLIC TRANSPORT Bus and train service to nearby Kingswood

REFRESHMENTS Navigation pub by Kingswood Bridge, Tom o' the Wood at Turner's Green and café for visitors to Baddesley Clinton

PUBLIC TOILETS Beside car park and at Baddesley Clinton for visitors to the house

ORDNANCE SURVEY MAP Explorer 220 (Birmingham, Walsall, Solihull & Redditch) and 221 (Coventry & Warwick)

canal, shortly entering a cutting. At the far end, go beneath another bridge and then climb the bank to cross it. Continue up the lane to the main road at Rowington.

B Cross to the churchyard opposite and follow a path around the northern side of the church to a stile beneath a large yew, waymarked 'Heart of England Way'. Go forward at the top of a field below the old vicarage and over another stile. Turn right and walk beside the hedge, continuing in the same direction when you reach the next field. At a stile on the far side, instead of crossing, turn left. Follow the hedge on your right until it turns away and then keep going across the open field. Over a stile in the far fence, a contained path leads out to a lane.

C Walk right and, at the end, go right again. A little distance along, however, turn off left onto a gated track, again signed 'Heart of England Way'. Walk ahead, passing Lyons Farm and on, shortly beside a wood. Beyond, where the track then turns left, leave ahead through a small gate. Keep going in the same direction from field to field, eventually emerging onto a wooded drive near Baddesley Clinton church. Left leads past the Church and on through trees to a drive at the entrance to the house.

Passing through the locks at Kingswood Junction

Foxgloves near Baddesley Clinton

D Follow the drive away from the house and past the visitor car park. A little farther on, where the private drive from the house merges, go over a stile on the left. A track heads away to follow the outer boundary of the gardens. Carry on over a stream and, later, a crossing track, eventually entering a large, sloping paddock. Bear right across to a gate and stile in the bottom corner by a stable at Clinton Farm, where a track leads out to the road.

E Go right past the Navigation pub and over the bridge, immediately dropping left onto the Grand Union Canal. Turn right, back to Kingswood Junction and, after crossing a bridge over the linking arm, double back beneath it to retrace your steps to the car park. ●

The Grand Union Company was formed in 1929, amalgamating canals owned by at least eight independent companies to form a unified waterway connecting Birmingham with London. It was conceived as a broad gauge canal capable of carrying 70-ton barges, but initially the 7-ft (2m) wide barges could travel only as far as **Braunston**. A programme to widen the narrow-boat canals of the Birmingham system was begun, but the cost proved prohibitive. With the outbreak of World War II, all development ceased and within 10 years, virtually all freight had moved onto the railways.

What decorates the massive chimney-piece in Baddesley Clinton's Great Hall?

19 *Brewood to Chillington Hall*

START Brewood Parish Church
DISTANCE 5½ miles (8.9 km)
TIME 3¾ hours
PARKING Roadside parking in village
ROUTE FEATURES Undemanding field paths, tracks and canal towpaths

Rolling countryside, a charming country house and park and delightful village combine to make this walk an ideal summer's day out. It concludes with a stretch beside the Shropshire Union Canal, where more often than not, you can watch colourful barges chugging by.

Leave the main street opposite the south-west corner of St Mary and St Chad's Church, along a waymarked alleyway beside Dean Cottage. Emerging onto a track at the bottom, cross into a paddock opposite and continue ahead over the fields towards Dean's Hall Bridge.

A Cross the canal and carry on along the track beyond for about ½ mile (800m). On reaching a junction, turn left on another track, signed to The Woolley and Hyde Farm, and then keep ahead at a crossing opposite Woolley Farm.

B Where the track then bends right, a little farther on, leave through a waymarked kissing-gate into a field on the left and walk away beside the left-hand hedge. At the far end, through another gate, carry on at the edge of a wood to reach the Upper Avenue leading from Chillington Hall. Bear right, crossing it to emerge onto a lane at the far side.

? *Three of the Gifford tombs have small figures carved around their bases, representing their children. How many did each have?*

PUBLIC TRANSPORT Bus service to Brewood
REFRESHMENTS Choice of pubs and a café in Brewood
PUBLIC TOILETS In Brewood
ORDNANCE SURVEY MAP Explorer 242 (Telford, Ironbridge & The Wrekin)

C Turn right and walk to the top. *Alternatively, to shorten the walk, turn off left almost immediately to continue across the fields on the Staffordshire Way rejoining the walk at point* **E**.

D The entrance to Chillington Park lies opposite the junction. However, the onward route is along the lane to the left. After some 250 yds (228m), turn off left onto a track, marked Chillington Street on the map, which eventually narrows to a grassy way.

E Keep going to the end of the track, emerging by some cottages onto a road. Cross to continue along Park Lane, opposite. Where that then bends sharply left, leave along a track on the right, which, after passing a couple of houses, heads on across the fields. After some 700 yds (639m), just after passing beneath power cables, turn through a gap into the field on the left and walk away beside the right-hand hedge. Carry on into the next field, shortly reaching the canal at Hunting Bridge.

Elegant Georgian buildings line the streets of the village, near to which, at Boscobel, Charles II hid in an oak tree following his defeat at the Battle of Worcester. His companion, Colonel William Carless, is buried near a yew tree in the churchyard of **St Mary and St Chad's**. Inside the church you will find some **magnificent alabaster tombs** of the Gifford family, the oldest dating from 1556, which display intricate detail of the elegant costumes of the day in their fine carving. There is also a fine memorial to the Moreton family.

Avenue Bridge crossing the Shropshire Union Canal

Avenue Bridge, number 10, carrying the formal tree-lined drive to **Chillington Hall** high above the waterway, stands out in contrast to the others passed along the way. Indeed, it is the grandest bridge on the whole of the Shropshire Union Canal and was built in 1826 to a design attributed to Thomas Telford.

F Drop right onto the canal towpath and follow it back beneath the bridge towards Brewood. Approaching Chillington Bridge, the canal passes into a wooded cutting, emerging ¾ mile (1.2km) farther on, just before Dean's Hall Bridge. Leave the canal there, and return along your outward route across the fields to Brewood. ●

Moreton family monument in Brewood church

Originating in Normandy, the **Giffards** (now spelt Gifford) came to England with **William the Conqueror** and were originally granted land in Wiltshire. The family acquired Chillington from its previous owner, Peter Corbeson, in 1178, paying for it the princely sum of '25 marks and a charger of metal'. The house at the centre of the Chillington estate is the third to have occupied the site and succeeds a 12th-century castle and a 16th-century manor. It was built during the 18th century, the design and decoration reflecting the plain, elegant style of its time. The landscaped park was laid out after the completion of the house by **'Capability' Brown**, and leads down to an expansive ornamental lake.

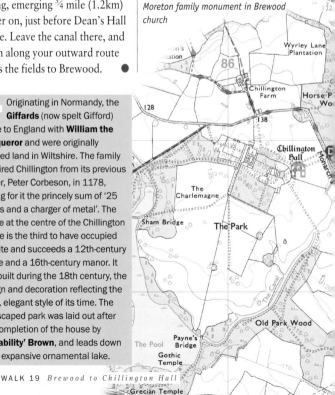

20 *Packwood House*

START Kingswood Junction
DISTANCE 5½ miles (8.9km)
TIME 3¼ hours
PARKING Car park at start of walk
ROUTE FEATURES Canal towpaths and field paths, a short distance along lanes

Although this walk is enjoyable at any time of year, come in early spring when the lawns in front of Packwood House are ablaze with gold, a carpet of countless daffodils. Another highlight is the long flight of locks that lifts the Stratford-upon-Avon Canal some 120 ft (36m) on its way into Birmingham.

🖉 The Stratford-upon-Avon Canal runs beside the car park. Follow it right to the first bridge, cross to the central island and bear left past a lock. Cross another bridge and follow a short stretch of canal beneath a railway bridge, linking it to the Grand Union.

Ⓐ Cross the bridge over the link and continue north along the towpath. Carry on beneath Kingswood Bridge for a farther ¾ mile (1.2km) to Rising Bridge, there climbing onto the road above. Walk left, on past a road junction and over a railway line.

Ⓑ Just beyond the bridge, turn right along a private road, The Grove. In front of a gate at the end, go right onto a path around the perimeter of the house and its garden, emerging at a drive beyond. Cross to a kissing-gate opposite and turn right along the edge of a field. Keep on over a lateral track and then pass by some barns into a yard at Uplands Farm. There, a track leads left to a lane.

? *On your walk back along the canal, how many locks are passed?*

PUBLIC TRANSPORT Bus and rail service to nearby Kingswood
REFRESHMENTS Seasonal ice cream van at Packwood House
PUBLIC TOILETS Beside car park and at Packwood House for visitors
ORDNANCE SURVEY MAP Explorer 220 (Birmingham, Walsall, Solihull & Redditch)

Near Lapworth on the Stratford-upon-Avon Canal

C Go right and then, almost immediately, left over a stile by a gate onto Packwood Avenue. Although the line of sight is broken by its passage through Gorse Wood, the avenue runs dead-straight for some 1200 yds (1100m) and is bordered on both sides by trees, as impressive an approach to a house as any. At the far end, leave through a wrought-iron gate onto the daffodil lawns that front Packwood House.

D The onward route lies along the lane to the left, passing the famous yew topiary garden. Carry on over a gentle rise until you reach a junction, there leave the lane, crossing a stile into the corner of a garden. Walk away, keeping to the right-hand edge of the lawn, and go past the side of the house to a field beyond. Continue ahead beside woodland into the next field and follow the boundary around to a stile. Cross into parkland at the rear of Packwood House and bear left, following waymarks to emerge onto a lane at the far side.

The **Packwood estate** was originally held by the Benedictine monks at Coventry, but with Henry VIII's Dissolution of the monasteries, it passed into secular hands. Packwood eventually came to the **Fetherstons**, who built the fine timber-framed, Tudor-style manor house towards the end of the 16th century. The upper part of the impressive yew gardens was laid out about 1650 by John Fetherston, but the southern part is thought to have been a 19th century addition to replace an old orchard. The house came to the National Trust as a gift in 1941 from the last owner, Mr Graham Baron Ash, son of the Birmingham industrialist Alfred Ash.

E A drive opposite leads to Malt House Farm. In front of the gates, pass through a gap on the left into a field and go right to find a stile in the corner. Over that, turn left and follow the hedge into the next field. Keep ahead, the field eventually narrowing and leading out to a road. Turn left, but then cross to a track leading to Draw Bridge Farm. However, instead of going over the 'drawbridge', swing left onto the towpath of the Stratford-upon-Avon Canal.

F Although there is still a fair way to go before the end of the walk, the way is easy and, in fact, down hill as you drop past a series of locks. By lock number 4, the third one you come to, the path crosses to the opposite bank, on which you should remain until you eventually reach the car park.

The **Stratford-upon-Avon Canal** was completed in 1816, having taken 10 years to build. It arrived in **Kingswood** in 1802, passing within yards of the Warwick and Birmingham Canal (now part of the Grand Union). Despite the fierce competition between the various canal companies, a link was built between the two, and Kingswood developed as a busy junction, a motorway interchange of its day. Although there was barely any difference in elevation between the two waterways, a lock was installed in the connecting cut to prevent one 'stealing' water from the other. This was, in fact, no petty detail, for the passage of a single barge through a lock uses some **25,000 gallons of water**, and when the canal was very busy, or there had been little rain, there was always a danger of the summit reaches running dry.

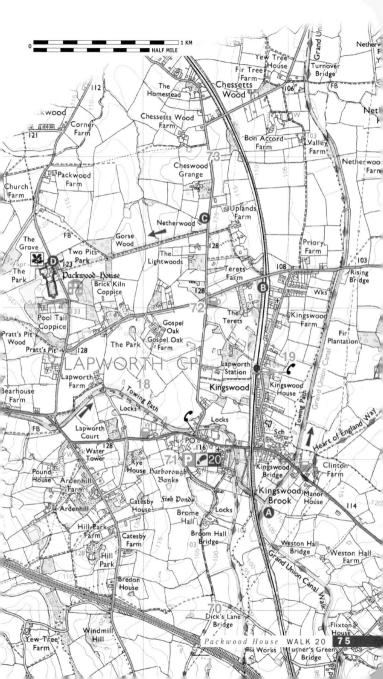

Further Information

Walking Safety

Always take with you both warm and waterproof clothing and sufficient food and drink. Wear suitable footwear, i.e. strong walking boots or shoes that give a good grip over stony ground, on slippery slopes and in muddy conditions. Try to obtain a local weather forecast and bear it in mind before you start. Do not be afraid to abandon your proposed route and return to your starting point in the event of a sudden and unexpected deterioration in the weather.

All the walks described in this book will be safe to do, given due care and respect, even during the winter. Indeed, a crisp, fine winter day often provides perfect walking conditions, with firm ground underfoot and a clarity of light unique to that time of the year.

The most difficult hazard likely to be encountered is mud, especially when walking along woodland and field paths, farm tracks and bridleways – the latter in particular can often get churned up by cyclists and horses. In summer, an additional difficulty may be narrow and overgrown paths, particularly along the edges of cultivated fields. Neither should constitute a major problem provided that the appropriate footwear is worn.

Abandoned rock house at Kinver Edge

Baddesley Clinton

Follow the Country Code

- Enjoy the countryside and respect its life and work
- Guard against all risk of fire
- Take your litter home
- Fasten all gates
- Help to keep all water clean
- Keep your dogs under control
- Protect wildlife, plants and trees
- Keep to public paths across farmland
- Take special care on country roads
- Leave livestock, crops and machinery alone
- Make no unnecessary noise
- Use gates and stiles to cross fences, hedges and walls

(The Countryside Agency)

Useful Organisations

British Waterways
The Stop House, Braunston, Northants NN11 7JQ.
Tel. 01788 890666; Fax 01788 890222; website: www.britishwaterways.co.uk

Council for the Protection of Rural England
128 Southwark St, London SE1 0SW.
Tel. 020 798 12800

Youth Hostels Association
Trevelyan House, Dimple Road, Matlock, Derbyshire DE4 3YH.
Tel. 01629 592600
Website: www.yha.org.uk

Council for National Parks
246 Lavender Hill,
London SW11 1LJ.
Tel. 020 7924 4077

Countryside Agency
John Dower House, Crescent
Place, Cheltenham GL50 3RA.
Tel. 01242 521381

English Heritage
23 Savile Row, London W1X 1AB.
Tel. 0171 973 3250; Fax 0171 973
3146; Website: www.english-
heritage.org.uk
Regional Office
West Midlands
Tel. 0845 3010 004

English Nature
Northminster House,
Peterborough PE1 1UA.

Tel. 01733 455100; Fax 01733
455103; E-mail:
enquiries@english-nature.org.uk;
Website: www.english-
nature.org.uk

National Trust
Membership and general enquiries:
PO Box 39, Bromley, Kent BR1
3XL.
Tel. 0181 315 111; E-mail:
enquires@ntrust.org.uk; Website:
www.nationaltrust.org.uk
Regional Office
West Midlands
Tel. 01743 708100

Ramblers' Association
2nd Floor, Camelford House,
87–90 Albert Embankment,
London SE1 7TW.
Tel. 020 7339 8500

Essex Bridge near Shugborough

Tourist Information

Heart of England Tourist Board
Woodside, Larkhill Road,
Worcester WR5 2EZ.
Tel. 01905 763436;
Fax 01905 763450

Local Tourist Information Centres

Bewdley: 01299 404740
Birmingham: 0121 693 6300
Bridgnorth: 01746 763257
Bromsgrove: 01527 831809
Droitwich Spa: 01905 774312
Kenilworth: 01926 852595/
850708
Redditch: 01527 60806
Solihull: 0121 704 6130
Stafford: 01785 240204
Stratford-upon-Avon: 01789
293127
Warwick: 01926 492212

Public Transport

For all public transport enquiries:
Traveline: 0870 608 2608

Ordnance Survey maps of Birmingham and the Heart of England

Explorer Maps: 204 (Worcester & Droitwich Spa), 205 (Stratford-upon-Avon), 218 (Wyre Forest & Kidderminster), 219 (Wolverhampton & Dudley), 220 (Birmingham), 221 (Coventry & Warwick), 242 (Telford & Ironbridge), 244 (Cannock Chase) and 245 (The National Forest).

Answers to Questions

Walk 1: Moscow and New York, almost due east and west respectively.

Walk 2: Walton Hill, it is 1 mile (1.6km) away and 1,036 ft (316m) high.

Walk 3: It is one of the unusual carvings on the pulpit.

Walk 4: The information panel in New Fallings Coppice has the answer, three; the green, great spotted and lesser spotted. You may hear them 'drumming', and if very lucky, even catch sight of them.

Walk 5: During the medieval period, people were required to give one-tenth of their income, or a 'tithe' to the Church. Farmers made their payment in kind and thus the grain had to be stored before being sold.

Walk 6: For cheapness, the bridges were built only as wide as the canal, and thus the draw horse had to pass around the outside. The split, however, allowed the towrope to be slipped through, thus avoiding the trouble of unharnessing the horse.

Walk 7: The fox shows four toes, while the badger has five. Look for the symbols marking the nature trails from the Visitor Centre.

Walk 8: The 1957 World Jubilee Jamboree, which was attended by more than 52,000 Boy Scouts.

Walk 9: 1701 – you will see the date set bold above the main entrance.

Walk 10: On 10 June 1967. It was established by a voluntary German organisation, the Volksbund, and groups of young people come to this country each year to help care for the graves.

Walk 11: Queen Elizabeth I.

Walk 12: Fourteen, but only six of them actually span the river, unless it is in flood.

Walk 13: Earlstown, near St Helens, by J S Lee and Co. It originally stood in a salt warehouse at Horninglow Basin, Burton.

Walk 14: Among the figures depicted are the baker, district nurse, fireman and butcher. You will also find the town crier, a local coach driver, and, of course, Jesus, shown as a carpenter.

Walk 15: Four battlemented turrets rise above its central tower.

Walk 16: 21 March 1914, in memory of the Revd John Heath Sykes who had served as the vicar for 45 years.

Walk 17: Rhododendron; native to Asia Minor, it was introduced into Britain around the end of the 17th century and often planted in woodland to provide cover for game. However, it is difficult to control and, despite its attractive flowers, is often regarded as a pest.

Walk 18: Shields depicting the coats of arms of the several families allied by marriage to the Ferrers.

Walk 19: 18, 17 and 14. Those shown wrapped in swaddling died at birth or in infancy.

Walk 20: 18, the first is lock number 2 and the last one, just above the car park, is number 19.